FESTIVALS and CELEBRATIONS

Chinese New Year

By Louise Nelson

KidHaven PUBLISHING

Published in 2023 by
KidHaven Publishing, an Imprint of Greenhaven Publishing, LLC
2544 Clinton St., Buffalo, NY 14224

Written by: Louise Nelson
Edited by: William Anthony
Designed by: Amy Li
Image Credits: All images are courtesy of Shutterstock.com. With thanks to Getty Images, Thinkstock Photo and iStockphoto.
Recurring images – Peratek (pattern), TinyDoz (character), curiosity, svetichstock, girafchik, Auspicious (vectors). Cover – Magnia, Lionger, Peratek, winphong, Artissara, OSABEE, Please Remember. 4–5 – hijodeponggol, Rawpixel.com. 6–7 – alexan888, Dan76, Kochkanyan Juliya. 8–9 – Kochkanyan Juliya, sub job, Lukasz Szwaj. 10–11 – PR Image Factory, ViewStock. 12–13 – Dragon Images, Tom Wang. 14–15 – Mcimage, Wirestock Creators, lukpedclub, Kochkanyan Juliya. 16–17 – Kochkanyan Juliya, Jinning Li, yuda chen. 18–19 – Ekkalak Ngamjarasvanij, windmoon. 20–21 – DMHai, jennipenni89. 22–23 – Mihai_Andritoiu, Kochkanyan Juliya, Lukasz Szwaj.

Cataloging-in-Publication Data

Names: Nelson, Louise.
Title: Chinese New Year / Louise Nelson.
Description: New York : KidHaven Publishing, 2023. | Series: Festivals and celebrations | Includes glossary and index.
Identifiers: ISBN 9781534543027 (pbk.) | ISBN 9781534543041 (library bound) | ISBN 9781534543058 (ebook)
Subjects: LCSH: Chinese New Year--Juvenile literature. | China--Social life and customs--Juvenile literature.
Classification: LCC GT4905.N45 2023 | DDC 394.261--dc23

Manufactured in the United States of America

CPSIA compliance information: Batch #CWKH23: For further information contact Greenhaven Publishing LLC at 1-844-317-7404.

Please visit our website, www.greenhavenpublishing.com.
For a free color catalog of all our high-quality books, call toll free 1-844-317-7404 or fax 1-844-317-7405.

Contents

Words that look like this can be found in the glossary on page 24.

What Is a Festival?

A festival is when people come together to celebrate something special or an important time of year. Some festivals last for just one day, and others are celebrated for many months.

There are lots of different festivals. Some festivals are celebrated with a big feast with friends and family. During some festivals, it is traditional to give presents to your friends and family.

Lots of festivals have music and dancing, and people might wear colorful costumes.

Chinese New Year

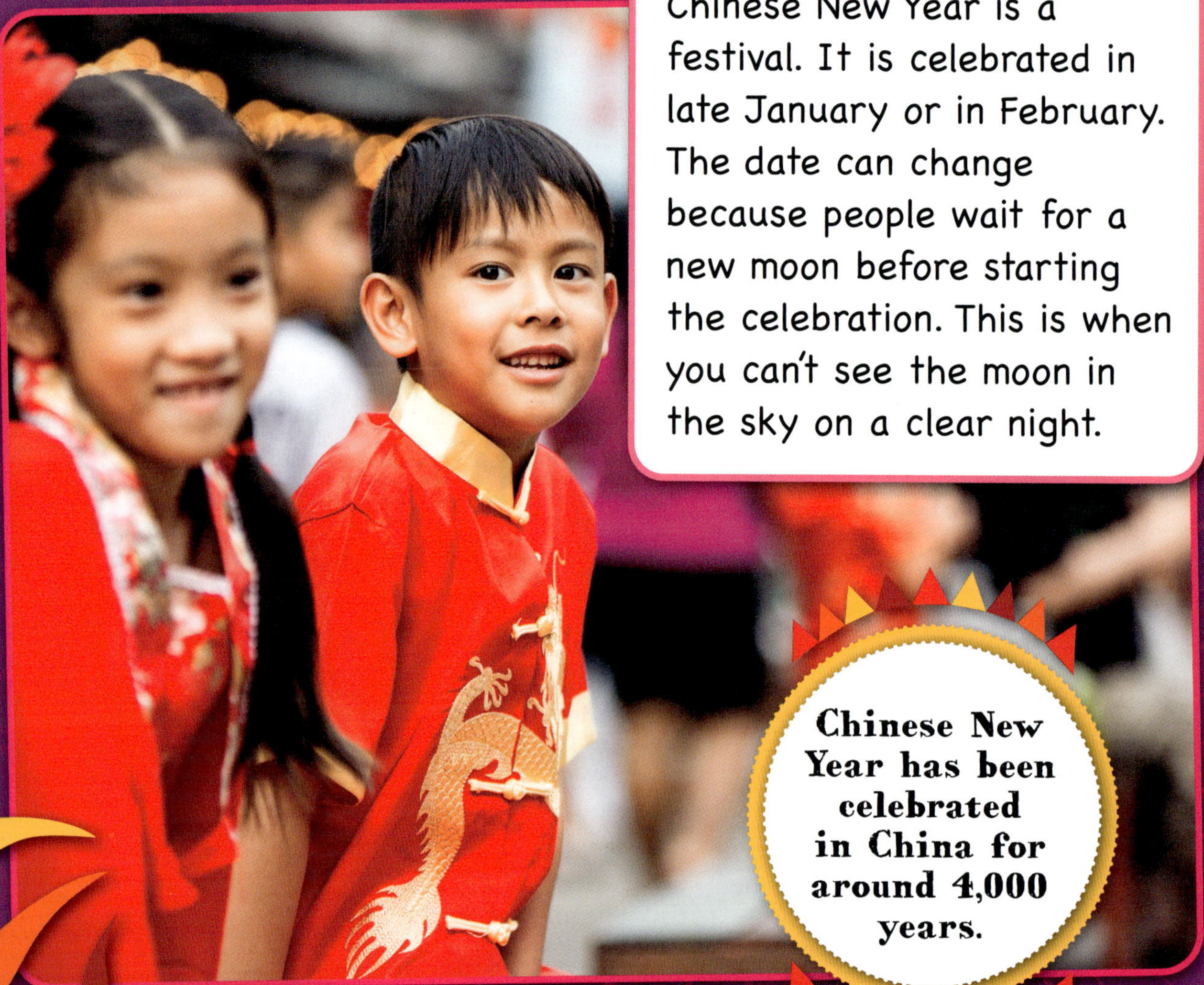

Chinese New Year is a festival. It is celebrated in late January or in February. The date can change because people wait for a new moon before starting the celebration. This is when you can't see the moon in the sky on a clear night.

Chinese New Year has been celebrated in China for around 4,000 years.

Chinese New Year is sometimes called the Spring Festival. Families come together and wish each other good fortune.

People remember their ancestors during Chinese New Year.

The Story

A long time ago, there was a monster called Nian. Nian lived high above a village, in the mountains.

Nian woke up on New Year's Day every year and attacked the village, scaring all the children. The monster ate all of the food and all of the animals.

Every New Year's Eve, the villagers would hide away from Nian in their houses in fear.

One year, an old man came to the village. He saw how scared the villagers were, so he stayed for three days to watch over them. On his last day, he told the villagers that Nian was frightened by loud noises and the color red.

So, on New Year's Eve, the villagers lit fireworks and <u>firecrackers</u>. They hung red <u>lanterns</u> in the streets and all the children wore masks.

Nian never came down from the mountains ever again. The villagers were safe from then on!

Before the Festival

Many people start getting ready for the festival about one week before New Year's Day. People get ready by cleaning their homes. It is important to get rid of any dust and bad luck.

People believe that red is a lucky color that brings them happiness and good fortune. Because of this, Chinese New Year decorations are usually red. People may hang decorations such as red lanterns.

Red is the color that scared away the monster Nian.

New Year's Eve

New Year's Eve is a day for family. Families spend New Year's Eve together, and many people have a big feast with lots of food.

Some people decorate their homes with poems called spring couplets. The poems are written on red paper and hung up in doorways.

New Year's Day

After the New Year's Eve feast, some people might stay up until <u>midnight</u>. At midnight, fireworks are lit and people set off firecrackers. Everything is colorful and loud to scare Nian away, just like in the story.

Xin Nian Kuai Le* means "Happy New Year" in Mandarin. Say: *shin nee-an kwai le.

People share gifts on New Year's Day. It is traditional to give special red envelopes to each other. The envelopes have money inside them, and people believe that this protects them from bad luck.

Some people send red envelopes to their friends on phone apps.

Food

In some parts of China, it is a tradition for families to make and eat dumplings together. The Chinese word for dumpling is *jiaozi* and they represent the changing of the year.

***Jiaozi* might have pork, beef, or vegetables inside.**

Some parts of China traditionally serve sweet rice balls during New Year. They are made from a special rice powder and filled with sugar, fruits, or nuts.

Lanterns

After New Year's Day, families may spend the next week visiting relatives and friends. The Lantern Festival begins when the next full moon arrives.

People go outside to see the beautiful lanterns and watch the impressive dragon dancers. Long dragons are carried on sticks and swirled around by dancers.

Zodiac Signs

When the new year starts, there will be a new zodiac sign. The zodiac signs are 12 animals. Each animal means a different thing.

People born in the year of the tiger are said to be <u>adventurous</u> and kind.

Can you find the year you were born?
What is your Chinese zodiac animal?

Rat

(1996, 2008, 2020)

Ox

(1997, 2009, 2021)

Tiger

(1998, 2010, 2022)

Rabbit

(1999, 2011, 2023)

Dragon

(2000, 2012, 2024)

Snake

(2001, 2013, 2025)

Horse

(2002, 2014, 2026)

Goat

(2003, 2015, 2027)

Monkey

(2004, 2016, 2028)

Rooster

(2005, 2017, 2029)

Dog

(2006, 2018, 2030)

Pig

(2007, 2019, 2031)

If you were born at the end of January or in February, you may need to double-check what your Chinese zodiac is.

Chinese New Year Around the World

Chinese New Year celebrations take place all around the world because many people who celebrate it live outside of China. There is a big celebration in New York in the U.S. every year with music, fireworks, and a parade.

Do any Chinese New Year celebrations happen where you live?

Quiz

What have you learned about Chinese New Year?

1. For how long has Chinese New Year been celebrated in China?

2. What is the monster from the Chinese New Year story called?

3. What do the red envelopes have inside them?

4. What are some festive foods eaten during Chinese New Year?

5. What marks the end of Chinese New Year celebrations?

Answers: 1. Around 4,000 years 2. Nian 3. Money 4. Dumplings and sweet rice balls 5. The Lantern Festival

Glossary

adventurous ready to explore and try new things

ancestors people in your family who lived a long time ago

costumes special clothes

firecrackers small tubes that make loud noises when lit

fortune a person's luck

lanterns lights covered in paper that come in different shapes

midnight twelve o'clock at night

parade when people walk or dance down a street with others watching

relatives members of the same family

traditional relating to a belief or action that is passed down between people over time

Index